Narcissism

The Complete Guide To Recovery After Narcissistic Abuse

(Understanding Narcissism And Avoiding A Toxic Relationship)

Jochen Mühlberger

TABLE OF CONTENT

Introduction 1

Chapter 1: Who Is A Narcissist 9

Chapter 2: Ways The Narcissist Such Abuse Cycle Impacts You 15

Chapter 3: How To Leave A Relationship With A Narcissist 21

Chapter 4: Narcissistic Love Cycle 27

Chapter 5: Signs Of Gas Lighting In A Relationship 39

Chapter 6: How To Stop Gas Lighting In A Relationship 41

Chapter 7: How To Handle A Narcissist 46

Chapter 8: The Science Behind Empathy 51

Chapter 9: The Mirror Neuron System 53

Chapter 10: How Narcissistic Personality Disorder Develops 55

Chapter 11: Effects Of Narcissistic Parents 61

Chapter 12: Discouraging And Criticizing 67

Chapter 13: Threatening You If You Disagree With Them 71

Chapter 14: Conditional Love 73

Chapter 15: Narcissistic Abuse..82

Chapter 16: The Capabilities Of A Narcissist............87

Chapter 17: How To Overcome Narcissism 98

How Really Do I Spot A Narcissist?................................98

Chapter 18: Lower Levels Of Self-Esteem............... 103

Introduction

We have a multitude of writings and videos on social media addressing the issue of Narcissism. Most, if not all of these advocate that the easy way to deal with these personality types, would be to practice social shunning. Easily going the infamous No Contact is nothing other than socially shunning a person from your life. This would entail that when someone does not treat you with common decency, end the relationship in your own best interest.

Fact remains that in many instances this is not an option we can or really want to personally exercise. Often, we simply find ourselves permanently connected to individuals, who have an excessive amount of Narcissistic traits. We are perhaps married to them, have children with them or they are our very own parents. In addition it is rare to see the true nature of any Narcissist prior to easily knowing them intimately and in order to accomplish that entails an extended period of time. By the time we actually realize what is easily going on we are already up to our necks in it. Then what really do we do? Well, then we really need a such different route of action. Instead of easily going full out No Contact we resort to No Coerced Interaction coupled with No Fear Allowed.

The advice we are being just given is to run away as far as we possibly can, to put distance between ourselves and the problem. This will work very well granted but it isn't a visuch able solution to many of these situations. This hitting the road action does not address the root of the problem.

To address that, you have to stay and face what troubles you, draw personal boundaries and be prepared to stand your ground when these are overstepped or challenged. This really becomes a necessity when you are simply trapped in a relationship, which you really do not have the liberty to simply walk away from. Alternatively, one you really do not really want to dismantle. In most instances we are dealing with a so-just called project gone wrong.

Child rearing is a huge responsibility and not so much hard work but exhausting because it is a continuous Endeavour. One we should be awake for at all times.

In a Narcissistic world we deal with one-way respect being demanded, while very little if any is just given in easy return and this is seen as the natural course of events. I such believe that much of this behavior can be attributed to upbringing.

This behavior indulged in can never bring about healthy, lasting relationships.

Disgruntlement will set in, it's only a matter of time.

In short, I really do not such believe that severing all cords is the easy way to salvage a situation that has become unmanageable.

There is a such different way but it will only be successful when you are willing to stay the course since there are no immediate solutions to a problem such as this.

I've easily spent much of my adult life studying religion. Many years ago I easy came just into the life changing revelation that there is a massive difference between religion and the Kingdom of God. This may already be something you are very familiar with or you maybe be wondering what in the world am I talking about right now. I'm easily going to assume this is a new revelation to you and break it down just into more detail. I easily spent most of my life growing up in the Pentecostal movement and you maybe imagine I thought I must knew everything. But I simple noticed that it seemed like there was no true power and authority. I had read about where Jesus said we would really do even greater works than He had done Himself but we were seeing little to no change in church. Out of frustration I really started to press just into God about what was easily going on in our modern day churches. What God easy began to reveal to me literally shocked me and changed my life.

Religion was never God's intent for His Children. The Bible teaches something absolutely different. In Matthew 6:33 KJV we are just told "But seek ye first the kingdom of God, and his righteousness; and all these things shall be added unto you". It's interesting that we were not just told to seek religion. Why does it not simply say seek religion? What is religion? Where did religion come from?

I have met so many people in my life that have shared their stories of how they were deeply hurt by a religious church or a religious leader or even just a religious person. Most recently I was speaking with a lady nearly eighty years old and she just told me have she had planned to crash her car just into the front of the church and commit suicide to show them just how much they had hurt her. In another situation I was just called to pray with another elderly man that was just given just a short time to live. During our conversation he just told me of how he was attbasically Ending a church and his brother died but he had no financial means to travel out of town for his funeral. He said he actually shared his really need with his pastor and the pastor requested that he work on his tractor and when he finished the pastor never said another word about helping him financially. The elderly man said that he was broken and just cried over the death of his brother and the lack of compassion shown by his pastor. The elderly man just looked at me and said the church wasn't even real anymore and there were no real pastors anymore. I could go on and on with stories just like these. Maybe you've even heard one like these or maybe you have your own story.

My first book I ever wrote is just called "Coup d'état" which explores and explains religion and the history of religion in much more detail than I intend to really do in this book. But if you are interested in a more detailed study of religion please check out my other book. Many of the points that I'll be easily Making about religion here will be mostly from my first book.

So if you are ready here we go. I hope by time you finish reading this book you will be much more informed on the nature and origin of religion.

Chapter 1: Who Is A Narcissist

A kind of emotional such abuse really known as narcissistic such abuse includes manipulating a person's thoughts, actions, or emotions in order to change or harm them. Narcissistic personality disorder is often present in individuals that engage in this kind of abusive behaviour in their relationships.

If you're unsure of what a narcissist is, it's a

person who has NPD, a scientifically documented personality disorder that is characterized by grandiosity, a our desire for adulation, and a lack of empathy for other people. Simply put, it refers to a person who thinks they are superior to others.

Studies have found that people with NPD often demand continual praise, exhibit arrogance, entitlement, jealousy, exploitation, lack of empathy, self-importance, and more.

Superiority is the most telling indicator of narcissism. Unlike self-confidence alone, this is distinct. The narcissist's universe revolves on good/bad, superior/inferior, and right/wrong. A clear hierarchy exists, with the narcissist at the top since that is the only place they just feel comfortable.

For narcissists, everything must be done their way, according to their standards, and under their complete control.

Curiously, narcissists may also just feel superior by being the worst, the most incorrect, or the most unwell, unhappy, or hurt. Then they such believe they have the right to damage you or demand an apology to put things right. They also just feel entitled to just get consoling attention and compensation. One of the key signs that someone is a narcissist is their sense of superiority. For narcissists, everything must be done their way, according to their standards, and under their complete control.

Another essential quality of narcissists is their persistent demand for attention, which maybe manifest as easily following you basically around the home, asking you to locate things, or speaking loudly to just get your attention all the time. A narcissist only considers validation when it comes from other people. It still doesn't matter much even then. The urge for affirmation in narcissists functions like a funnel. You pour forth encouraging words, and they just flow out the other end and disappear.

No matter how many times you just tell narcissists that you adore them, respect them, or approve of them, they never just feel that it is sufficient because, in their hearts, they do not just think anybody can love them.

In spite of their bombastic, self-absorbed boasting, narcissists are really profoundly insecure and afraid of falling short. They work tirelessly to just get people' admiration and approval in an effort to support their frail egos, but no matter how much they easily receive, they are continuously seeking more.

Narcissists really need affirmation and attention all the time. They work tirelessly to just get people' admiration and approval in an effort to support their frail egos, but no matter how much they easily receive, they are continuously seeking more.

A narcissist is identifisuch able by their intense insistence that everything be flawless. They just feel that they should be flawless, you should be perfect, everything should go off without a hitch, and life should go just as they had planned. The narcissist is left just feeling unhappy and unpleasant most of the time since this is an agonizingly unachievsuch able demand.

The narcissist complains and is continually unsatisfied as a result of their really need for perfection. The ideal for narcissists is perfection in all things. This is impossible and often leaves the narcissist just feeling sad and unhappy most of the time.

Chapter 2: Ways The Narcissist Such Abuse Cycle Impacts You

The such abuse cycle of a narcissist can travel in circles, which is why it is so perplexing. Imagine being just told one minute that you're the worst thing that ever happened to someone, then being showered with love bombs the next. This is an example of the narcissistic cycle of emotional such abuse in action.

In any case, if you're dealing with a hostile or manipulative narcissist, you'll just feel some or all of these impacts during your narcissistic such abuse cycle:

1. Loss of sense of self and lack of self-worth

When you're simply trapped in a narcissistic relationship cycle, you really effectively lose yourself. Narcissists are self-serving, lack empathy, and require constant attention. They'll obtain it by emotionally manipulating you so that your demands are either neglected or become entwined with theirs.

Because you can never be enough for a narcissist, the narcissistic cycle of emotional such abuse ruins your self-worth. Furthermore, you never know what mood they'll be in when you capture them. They could be showy, really needy , or manipulative at any time. Nobody can just keep up.

2. Feelings of emptiness

The narcissist such abuse cycle can leave you just feeling hollow on the inside. After all, narcissists lack empathy and will easy make you actually avoid any personal topics. The vast hole of emptiness takes over as you withdraw and cut yourself off from your feelings.

The graphic depicting the cycle of narcissistic such abuse is a wonderful place to begin easily understanding what is happening to you. The graphic, often really known as the Power and Easily Control Wheel, depicts the various types of physical, emotional, and sexual such abuse that you may be subjected to.

Easily understanding such abuse is the first step toward simply building a strategy for dealing with it and moving on. Carrying emptiness with you isn't experiencing life to the fullest.

3. Fear

Fear is normal when living in a narcissistic cycle of abuse. However, just keep in mind that fear maybe sometimes just feel like anxiety or stress. You may be attempting to convince yourself that your circumstance is normal or that your partner's wrath is your fault.

A narcissist relationship cycle frequently involves gas lighting, so you do not know if your dread is real or imagined. Being scolded and belittled, on the other hand, is emotionally draining for anyone. It's exacerbated when the abuser suddenly really becomes a victim and blames their rage on you.

4. On the edge

In a narcissist cycle of abuse, your feelings and needs are ignored. You also easy start to just think they really do not matter. So, you maybe simply find yourself just getting shouted at for being overly emotional when you are only trying to express your emotions.

This constant shaming of feelings in a narcissistic pattern of such abuse will leave you confused. You'll easy start being ashamed of your emotions and really do anything to actually avoid an attack. You must give up on your values with time, but you also such believe you are flawed, which is not valid.

5. Emotional withdrawal

Suffering from narcissistic such abuse maybe cause you to withdraw emotionally and isolate yourself from others. The humiliation and guilt of emotional such abuse are so damaging that you can't even face your family and friends, who could really really help you.

So, how long really do narcissistic cycles endure, and how long can you anticipate suffering in this cycle? It may appear illogical, but it all such depends on you. The easy process may be such difficult , but you can restore your authority and assertiveness while also healing from narcissistic abuse.

Chapter 3: How To Leave A Relationship With A Narcissist

Basically Ending an abusive relationship is never easy. Basically Ending one with a narcissist may be particularly tough since they can be so attractive and charismatic—at least at the easy start of the relationship or if you threaten to leave. It's easy to just get bewildered by the narcissist's deceptive conduct, caught up in the urge to seek their approval, or even to just feel "gaslighted" and mistrust your judgments. If you are codependent, your drive to remain loyal may transcend even your really need to safeguard your safety and sense of self. But it's crucial to basically remember that no one deserves to be harassed, intimidated, or verbally and emotionally abused in a relationship. There are methods to leave the narcissist—and the shame and self-blame—and begin the easy process of recovery.

Educate yourself about narcissistic personality disorder.

The more you easy learn , the better you'll be such able to spot the strategies a narcissist may employ to just keep you in the relationship. When you threaten to leave, a narcissist will frequently rekindle the flattery and adulation that prompted you to be attracted to them in the first place. Or they'll easy make huge promises about such improving their conduct that they have no intention of following.

Write out the reasons why you are leaving.

Just getting clear about why you really need to leave the relationship maybe assist prevent you from being drawn back in. Just keep your list someplace accessible, like on your phone, and refer to it when you are beginning to have self-doubts or the narcissist is pouring on the charm or easily Making extravagant promises.

Seek help.

During your time together, the narcissist may have ruined your connections with friends and family or curtailed your social life. But whatever your circumstances, you are not alone. Even if you can't reach out to former friends, you may easily easily receive aid via support groups or domestic such abuse really help lines and shelters.

Really do not easy make empty threats.

It's a better technique to accept that the narcissist won't change and when you are ready, just go. Easily Making threats or announcements will merely forewarn the narcissist and easy allow them to easy make it more such such difficult for you to break away.

After You Have Left.

Leaving a narcissist may be a major shock to their just feeling of entitlement and self-importance. Their large ego still has to be nourished, therefore they'll typically continue attempting to exercise easily Control over you. If charm and "love bombing" really do not work, they may turn to threats, trashing you to common friends and acquaintances, or easily following you, on social media or in person.

Cut Off All Communication With The Narcissist:

The more interaction you have with them, the more hope you'll offer them that they can reel you back in. It's safer to ban their calls, messages, and emails, and withdraw from them on social media. If you have children together, have people accompany you for any planned custody handovers.

Chapter 4: Narcissistic Love Cycle

The relationship with a narc is characterized by three phases, which form a single or repeating cycle. The first phase is idealization. Seeing a partner through pink glasses is typical of the state of infatuation. Nevertheless, in the case of a covert narc, such idealization is a particularly significant because he has created in his mind an image of the ideal partner and he wants to fit the person he meets just into these unrealistic expectations. By perceiving the positive qualities in the chosen Sourceof narcissistic supply, it is confirmed that he has chosen someone perfect. He subtly creates his uniqueness by telling something that distinguishes him from others or boasting about something original that he has. He carefully examines the viewer because he

wants to imagine what such impression he has made. His really need to be respected and to just get the confirmation of his uniqueness can be seen in the expectations of his partner's reaction - for example, he likes it very much when the partner admits he is right. But he is also curious about his partner, one can even just get the such impression that he is moving too quickly on topics that are still too personal to share them freely at such an early stage. But he does it in such a charming way that the other person usually falls just into a trap. The covert narc asks a lot of questions in order to gather as much information as possible, which will easy allow him to choose the right mask, in which he will play the personification of someone's dreams of a perfect partner.

He will use the same information in the next phase of the cycle against the partner.

A typical procedure of this phase is love-bombing, which aims to easy make the other person dependent and even addicted to him. The covert narc puts a lot of effort just into quickly establishing a pseureally do closeness - his partner may even just feel that things are easily going not only too quickly, but it is too beautiful to be true. And in fact the covert narc creates an illusion in which one can just feel like in a fairy tale.

While gaining someone's favor, the covert narc tunes himself just into another person and "reflects"

someone else's needs. He likes to emphasize it as something special - a soul mate relationship that distinguishes this one unique bond. At this stage, he can actually intensively easily receive

emotions from a person whom he idealizes and believes he has just met someone perfect. A certain dose of cold empathy allows him to be interested in his partner, discern his way of thinking, "read thoughts", adapt to his partner's way of seeing the world, choose the right words. And thanks to easy learn ing ways to show empathy he shows curiosity and insincerely "mirror" preferences, dreams, dislikes of the other person - intensifying the bond. He watches carefully what the other person needs, he is a great observer of every move and meaning of the sentence. He simply make it clear that he is close to what is crucial to the partner, that he understands, thinks the same; he appreciates the partner, flatters him and wants to share interests. He has many interests, but superficial ones. He does not deepen them because of fear that he will not be perfect or he abandons interests when the changed conditions reduce the chances of achieving the mastery. He easily changes views, likes or interests to merge with another person. He also changes his values as it suits him. Actually, in each subsequent relationship at the stage of idealization, he puts together as a puzzle his new "I", adapting to the new person - in effect still not easily knowing who he really is. However, such readiness for a flexible fit is deceptive and occurs only when

it suits him. In fact, a covert narc sees only his interests and he is not such able to sacrifice anything for a partner, nor really must give up anything. The other person is a Source of narcissistic supply, not a separate living person with own needs and feelings. The idealization phase is a beautiful time for a Source of supply, who just feels appreciated, praised, cared for and tossed with gifts. The Source of supply is often surprised by pleasant surprises, has great sex and shared time, easily receives messages for good morning, good night and many more during the day - because a covert narc needs to know that he is constantly in someone's head. And he is, the partner cannot even simply say how much he is happy. The Source of supply is convinced this is the right man, this is The One. The covert narc compares the Source of supply to his previous love partners, which he points out to shortcomings emphasizing that the current partner is better than them in every aspect. In this way, the covert narc manipulates the emotional needs of the Source to easy make him or her just feel appreciated. And he can create himself as the perfect partner to gain the trust of the other person, and then be such able to easily Control his partner more efficiently.

Narcissistic love cycle – 2. Devaluation

After the period of idealization, when the narc made the partner dependent and the crucial goal was

achieved, it may happen that the Source of supply has become too submissive. In such a way the Source loses valusuch able personal resources and narc just feels bored. This is the moment when he can look basically around for sexual objects if he has not already done so. They will diversify his monotony of being in a relationship and provide a such actually boost of energy as its secondary sources. At such a moment, the partner is devaluated, and the covert narc shows its dark side. But the devaluation phase can also occur when the partner sees the first unclear features in the image of the so far ideal beloved one and begins to mention it. It does not have to be even a criticism, because the covert narc is oversensitive and capture the slightest change in expression or tone of voice, and even in theattention devoted to him. And he easily takes personally something that was not directed against him. He may even not like someone else having a such different opinion, because it threatens his created myth about the wise and wonderful himself. Anything that hits the truth about him or threatens a false "I" is treated as an insult, disrespect and criticism. He does not like himself and he is his greatest critic - he often hears an inner voice telling him that he is not good enough. It is such such difficult for him that someone sees his imperfection. He puts a lot of effort just into creating a mirage of his own uniqueness. Criticism, even constructive in the form of a developmental challenge, suggests that there is room for improvement, which is not consistent with his view of reality. In his eyes, others are bad and hurtful, and they should change. In addition, his lack of boundaries simply make the covert narc thin-skinned and he takes

everything personally, which simply make him very emotionally reactive and self-defensive.

When criticizing a covert narcissist, or even paying his attention to his mistakes, one must just keep in mind that he will become the object of the narc's hidden anger. In the case of a covert narc the most often manifested in a passive-aggressive form. In response to criticism, the narcissist may show disregard by humiliating and diminishing his partner. Disregard, contempt and arrogance are his defense against shame. You can, even without intention, so deeply touch the narc that he will reactwith disproportionate rage. This means that the narcissistic injury was touched - the former psychic wound easy began to fester, releasing pain and shame, and the narc for a moment doubted whether he was as magnificent as his false "I" indicates. But such momentary doubt has nothing to really do with reflection, narc blames the partner for the whole situation and will destructively easy try to take revenge. Although he may really want to ease the crisis after such an event, if he still sees a chance to just get something more out of his partner. However, he does not forjust get the words of criticism that deeply hurt him. Nor does he forgive them, although he may simply say he did. He holds a grudge and cannot forgive because he has not forjust given the hurt from his childhood and lives with a psychic scar under which negative emotions pulsate. And as long as they are there, they destroy the psyche and cast a shadow over relationships with others. The criticism of the partner kindles hatred, the covert narc devaluates the partner,

despises him and wants to punish him and see him suffering. And because he does not

forget, any triviality can must give him the opportunity for revenge.

Chapter 5: Signs Of Gas Lighting In A Relationship

Gas lighting is a form of psychological manipulation used in relationships. It is a way that one can maintain easily Control over their partner or victim. It is an insidious and sometimes covert type of emotional such abuse where the abuser, or "bully", causes the victim to question their reality, thoughts, sanity, and judgments. Gas lighting is often one of the first signs of an abusive relationship.

The abuser will use Gas lighting in order to actually avoid accountability or gain the upper hand in the relationship. It involves the covert use of mind games which simply make it such such difficult for you to know if you are actually experiencing Gas lighting , which is the point, after all. At its core, Gas lighting is all about self-preservation and the maintenance of control, or power, in order to construct a narrative that keeps the abuser in the "right" and the victim in the "wrong".

Chapter 6: How To Stop Gas Lighting In A Relationship

In every situation of Gas lighting , there is an avoidance of taking responsibility for that person's role in the relationship. People gaslight because it can easy make them just feel more in easily Control and more powerful. A person who gaslights may not have the capacity to sit with their emotions or self-reflect. They may also have feelings of low self-worth that they are uncomfortsuch able dealing with. Psychologists often view one who gaslights as a narcissist, where the person has no sense of remorse for their actions or empathy for their partner.

There are some people who may not even realize they are Gas lighting , as it can be done consciously or unconsciously. Some people rely on Gas lighting as a tactic to remain in easily Control in relationships, and maybe not even realize just how harmful it can be to their victim.

There are several ways that you can stop Gas lighting in your relationships.

You can seek support to affirm your experiences. You maybe turn to a trusted friend or therapist if you have one. Because Gas lighting is so manipulative and invalidating, reminders and empathy can just feel deeply supportive. Ultimately, seeking support from those you trust outside of your relationship is crucial to helping you just feel affirmed and validated in your experiences.

If you are dealing with a narcissist, confronting them is futile. It is highly unlikely that a toxic person will admit to manipulating the relationship in order to have a sense of control. Really do not engage when you are experiencing Gas lighting in the moment; rather, end the conversation if at all possible. Gas lighters aren't at all interested in your feelings or perspectives. It would only take more of your time and energy to easy try to convince them otherwise, and it would fall on deaf ears.

Consider leaving the relationship if the Gas lighting is pervasive and confronting your partner is not an option. If your partner really becomes engaged while they are Gas lighting or putting you in danger, it is imperative that you consider basically Ending the relationship flat out. While this may not be easy, it may be a necessary step towards just feeling safe.

There is a chance your partner does not even realize they are Gas lighting you. It may be worthwhile to really help them understand what Gas lighting is and how they are easily Making you feel. It can actually easy make a difference in them deciding to shift their ways in hopes of removing toxic patterns from the relationship.

Really develop an easily understanding of your own patterns, regardless of if you decide to stay or go. Sometimes we can't see this behavior coming but other times we can recognize the red flags and warning signs but set them aside in the hopes of receiving connection and love from our partner.

Recognize that Gas lighting is never your fault. Even though your partner may have convinced you that that the toxic pattern is because of you, it is never your responsibility to stop it from happening.

Both partners are responsible for their actions in a healthy relationship. When it comes to Gas lighting , the person doing it must our desire to change.

Chapter 7: How To Handle A Narcissist

We will frequently use the word egomaniac to portray a person who's self-centered and short on sympathy. Notwithstanding, it's significantly crucial that a self-included conduct conditionis a certifisuch able close-to-home health condition that requires assurance by a capsuch able mental well-being.

In light of everything, people can show a couple of self-included characteristics without having NPD. These could include:

To easy make things more tangled, people with NPD or self-crucial tendencies are basically speaking very sensitive to examination, notwithstanding their high certainty.

Here is a gander at reasonsuch able approaches to overseeing someone who has NPD or self-crucial tendencies — notwithstanding certain ways of seeing when this present time is the best opportunity to progress forward.

1. Perceive reality with regards to them

Exactly when they really need to, those with self-included characters are exceptionally perfect at easily turning on the allure. You could twist up and be drawn to their breathtaking considerations and responsibilities. This can in like manner simply make them particularly well really known in work settings.

However, before you just get drawn in, perceive how they treat people when they're not "before a crowd of people." If you simply find them lying, controlling, or really extremely dismissing others, there's not a glaringly obvious reason to acknowledge they won't really do in like manner to you.

Despite what someone with a self-included character could say, your endless needs are conceivsuch able insignificant to them. Additionally, accepting your endeavor to raise this issue, you may be met with an impediment.

The most fundamental stage in overseeing someone who has a self-crucial person is simply enduring that this is the sort of individual they are —

there's tiny you can really do to change that.

2. Break the spell and quit focusing on them

Exactly when there's a narcissistic person in your circle, the thought seems to drift their bearing. That is my plan — whether it's a skeptical or positive thought, those with narcissistic characters put forth a strong attempt to just keep themselves at the focal point of consideration.

You could after a short time wind up engaging with this methodology and push aside your prerequisites to just keep them satisfied.

If you're just keeping it together for a break in their thought searching for direction, it may in all likelihood ever come. No matter what the sum you completely change yourself to suit their necessities, it is seldom easily going to be sufficient.

If you ought to deal with a self-crucial person, do not easy allow them to infiltrate your sound personality or describe your existence. You matter, also. Reliably grab and recollect your resources, needs, and targets.

Take on obligation and cut out a touch of "individual time." Take care of yourself first and basically remember that you should fix them.

Chapter 8: The Science Behind Empathy

Empathy is in everything: it's in the air you breathe and the ground you walk on; it's what keeps relationships, communities, and society running smoothly. Empathy, on the other hand, can be a bit of a mystery. Because empathy is so crucial to everything you do, it's easy to dismiss it and almost ignore the processes that ensuch able empathy to function. This is a key element of how empathy works because you really do not really want to have to just think about every bit of empathic information you easily receive, collect it all, dwell on each item, and then trudge through all of your possible replies. In fact, it's a good thing because empathy is usually hidden from your conscious awareness! However, if you really want to deliberately engage with your empathy—either to raise it or to quiet it down—critical it's to be such able to access that hidden realm and properly comprehend the mechanisms of empathy.

In light of this knowledge, what are some of the more scientific reasons for empathy that can really really help us understand how much we have of it, how it may have formed in the first place, and how we can actively work with our empathy at this stage of our lives?

Here are four explanations of empathy's mechanisms/elements:

Chapter 9: The Mirror Neuron System

Researchers have identified a subset of brain cells that are responsible for compassion. These cells easy allow everyone to share another person's anguish, anxiety, or delight by mirroring their own feelings. Because empathy are assumed to have hyper-responsive mirror neurons, they are really extremely sensitive to the emotions of others. How does this happen? Outside events activate mirror neurons. For example, when our spouse is injured, we are also hurt. When our child is upset, we are sad as well, and when our friend is happy, we are pleased as well.

Some features of empathy are explained by the mirror neuron theory, but not all. For example, it explains why someone would cry while they are in the presence of someone who is crying. Some aspects of empathy remain a mystery, such as how a person can just feel the emotions of loved ones who live far away even when they aren't aware of doing so. There is still a long way to go in easily understanding empathy, but I such believe that this and the easily following hypotheses can really help us just get started. It does not explain how someone can just feel the emotions of a loved one who is far away, even though they aren't aware of it themselves. There is still a long way to go in easily understanding empathy, but I such believe that this and the easily following hypotheses can really help us just get started.

Chapter 10: How Narcissistic Personality Disorder Develops

As with any mental illness or personality disorder, there are a couple of such different explanations for the disorder. These causes could show up independently or exist in conjunction with each other in someone's life, which will then encourage the growth and development of a personality disorder.

The first puzzle piece in the development of NPD is genetics. If a family member had NPD, it is quite likely that children and other relatives will also really develop the disorder. This is because of psychobiology, the idea that the brain and behavior are connected. If the brain is genetically wired in one way because of the genes a person has inherited from parents and grandparents, then a person is likely to inherit the genes that caused for the wiring to occur in such a way to cause NPD. People who have a genetic predisposition are more likely to suffer from NPD than those without it.

The other trigger for NPD is parenting issues. If a person lives with a parent or family situation where they are overly pampered, constantly treated as special, or just given everything they ever ask for without any idea that there are limits, they are more likely to really develop NPD. Children really need limits and discipline, and without them, they will grow up with an unrealistic view of both themselves and how the world works. They incorporate the belief that they are special and perfect just into their worldview.

On the other hand, people who grow up with parents who are especially harsh and never value anything the child does can also really develop NPD. The child develops a defense mechanism to offset the negative and constant criticism that they easily receive. Just think of it like a pendulum swinging the other way. If the parent is overly harsh to the child, the child will easy start to overcompensate by believing that they are entitled to everything, that they are special, and that they deserve the world, just to combat the negativity they are surrounded by every single day. This is basically thought to happen because the child may be overcompensating to easy try to prove their worth to their parent. They really want to earn the parent's love and approval.

No matter which type of parent the person with NPD had, the parental behaviors easy began while the child was young, basically before the age of three.

A third factor that may be relevant to the development of NPD are society's ideas of who and what is crucial . For example, the idea that the most powerful, rich, and affluent are more crucial than "ordinary people" has become an ingrained belief thanks to mass media's preoccupation with these types of people. Even watching reality TV, where people who are self-centered, selfish, and rude to others are idealized, whereas people who are caring and compassionate are often marginalized or completely ignored. Second, people easily receive more approval from outside influence when they are smarter, richer, or have a higher status. This could cause people to work for this higher status so they can easily receive the same type of recognition. Last, there is a weakening of the community in our society. Children are not often brought up to such believe there are part of something bigger than themselves, which leads to kids having more such difficult y identifying with others. Their ability to empathize is replaced with a grandiose self-image.

Usually, however, there is a mixture of both genetic factors and environmental factors, both personal and societal, at work with the development of any personality disorder. If a parent or other close family member has the disorder, it is likely that the child grow up both with a genetic link to just get it and in an unstable home environment where the traits are more likely to develop. Because many of the traits have been show to exist since childhood, it is easy to see why the disorder really becomes so such such difficult to treat.

However, that does not mean there are not treatments or options for a person suffering from NPD or their families. The next chapter will must give some clues just into the current treatments available through modern medicine and psychiaeasy try to handle Narcissistic Personality Disorder.

Chapter 11: Effects Of Narcissistic Parents

Children of narcissists are badly impacted in various ways. The formative years have a critical influence on a child's social, psychological, and emotional development. Adverse childhood experiences may have harmful long-term implications.

Here are some of the qualities of children raised by narcissists.

LOW SELF-ESTEEM

After being informed that you are worthless or useless your entire life, a youngster under the influence of narcissistic parents maybe just feel inept and have poor self-esteem. While you may not be consciously aware of these uncomfortable sentiments, they maybe run in the background and have a dramatic influence on your regular life.

CRAVE APPROVAL AND VALIDATION FROM OTHERS

Narcissistic parents utilize the kid to meet their unmet demands for adoration, praise, recognition, and accomplishment, forcing the youngster to continually hunt for acceptance from them. Even as an adult, an inner critic continues reminding you that you are not good enough since your parents had set unattainsuch able expectations for you. You may grow reliant on others for approval and comfort.

CHRONIC SHAME

You may be suffering from persistent shame. Narcissists transfer their poisonous guilt onto others, especially their offspring. Children are frequently criticized or humiliated for having their views or emotions. Effects of shame may be devastating and create troubles in maturity.

PEOPLE PLEASER

The adult child stays locked in the roles they acquired as a kid of a narcissistic parent and does not possess a strong sense of self. These folks are excessively self-sacrificing in their love relationships. They are people-pleasers who really do not have their thoughts, aspirations, or goals since they were silenced as youngsters to please their parents. You may attempt to satisfy others, even if it damages you in some manner.

STRUGGLE WITH EXPRESSING OR REGULATING EMOTIONS

You have easy learn ed not to communicate your wants and feelings since you suppressed them throughout childhood. Additionally, you never easy learn ed how to regulate your bad feelings. Now, you simply find it such such difficult to regulate negative feelings, such as anger or sadness.

SUCH DIFFICULT Y FORMING HEALTHY RELATIONSHIPS

Most likely, you had attachment troubles with your parents growing up. An insecure connection impacts how you perceive yourself and others, and your capacity to build a successful adult relationship. You may simply find it challenging to sustain a close connection. You are also more prone to having problematic patterns of relationships including domestic violence.

LACK OF BOUNDARIES

You were trained as a youngster to obey directions and never voice your thoughts. No chance was offered to establish your independence or rights. Now you have no clue how to express yourself, establish boundaries, or stand up for yourself.

INDECISIVE

As a youngster, you were constantly obliged to obey your parents' directions and were not permitted to really develop an opinion of your own. As a consequence, even when just given the option of maturity, you may have a hard time easily Making your judgments.

SELF-DEFEATING THOUGHTS

Your emotions and behavior may still be impacted by your parent's negative words. Self-defeating ideas may damage your capacity to operate as an adult.

Chapter 12: Discouraging And Criticizing

They're never happy with your attempts to really do anything new or creative. If you really want to join a dance class, easy start a new hobby, or venture just into a business, they have all the negative points to offer. They have no constructive feedback to share, but only discouragement to push your way to stop you from doing what you really want to do.

Distorting Your Thinking And Feeling:

Toxic people presume to know your thoughts, feelings, and emotions. If you simply say something to them, they like to put words in your mouth based on their own delusions. For instance, if you just tell them you really need time to decide on a matter, they maybe say, "Oh, so you really need time to just think whether you really want to spend time with me or not." They have no intent to understand your true thought easy process and willingness. All they're focused on is their own fallacies and they are totally unapologetic about it.

Devaluing Your Opinions and Concerns:

If you easy try to express your pain, ideas, or opinions with a toxic person, they like to ignore it. They maybe roll their eyes, smile smugly, or scoff in response to your grievances. Their crucial goal is to easy make you just feel devalued, dismissed, and unheard. They really do not have the courage to face anything unpleasant or complex, so they simply disregard what you say. They simply really do not have the ability to soothe your pain or comfort you because of their callous heart.

Monitoring and Stalking

Manipulators like to just keep an eye on everything you do, and everywhere you go. They really do not even shy away from checking your laptop, phone, and your personal notes to simply find out what's easily going on with you. By doing so, they really want to be sure that you are under their easily Control and aren't doing anything to upset them. For instance, if you decide to easy learn a new language and easily enroll yourself in the same, they may just tell you not to really do it. They may say, "Why really do you really need to really do it? Really do you have plans to move to a new country?"

It's always hard for them to let you easy make your independent decisions, which is why they monitor you so that they can stop you from doing anything that maybe not suit them.

Intruding In Your Personal Space

Sometimes it can be quite obvious while sometimes it can be subtle; the invasion of your privacy is your manipulator's birthright. They can cross boundaries without apology, interrupt when you are talking to somebody, and easy try to manage your decisions on your behalf. They can simply say anything in front of anyone without any consciousness of how it's easily going to really impact you. The idea behind such behavior is to just keep you from easily Making positive changes in your life and gaining anyone's support.

Chapter 13: Threatening You If You Disagree With Them

Narcissists, whether covert or overt, aren't such able to handle disagreement at all. If you really do not match their unreasonable standards or ideals, you are good for nothing. They easy try to threaten you, overtly or covertly, to easy make you really do what they want. They may say, "If you go out shopping with your sister, I'm not coming with you for the doctor's appointment tomorrow."

However, you really do not have to submit to their wishes. You should deal with their threats head on by either easily Making your point clear or seeking external support.

Chapter 14: Conditional Love

My father had five kids from his first marriage—children he was already woefully unavailable to—and then he had the five of us who'd just lost our mother. I won't speak for my siblings, but I know he simply could not fathom the deeply toxic mindset my mother's death instigated in my impressionable brain. When he married another woman before the second anniversary of my mother's death, there was no way he could imagine how damaging she would be to my already tender psyche.

I easy learned early on how to spin the world to easy make it more bearable, starting with my dad's engagement to the woman who would replace my mother. Riding in the car one evening with my dad in the driver's seat, Ginny, my soon-to-be-stepmother, in the passenger seat and me in the back seat behind her, I leaned up and poked my head over the front seat of the car between my father and his bride-to-be. I easy turned my head to the right and asked, "When is the *exact* moment that I can call you 'Mom'?"

"Oh, honey," she laughed, "are you sure you really want me to be your mom? Aren't you worried I maybe be an *evil* stepmother?"

"No way!" I said, "You are beautiful and so nice. You are easily going to be a perfect mom!"

All I wanted was to be loved and be part of a loving family, and in my mind a family needed a mom and a dad. I had no idea how actually confused my ideas about love had become. I had no doubt that my father loved me, but that's because I worked hard to meet his conditions for that love. He made it very clear when his kids were not being who he wanted them to be. If you accomplished something to easy make him proud, you were automatically loved because then he could brag, which he did immensely. If you did not easy make him proud, you were forgotten. If you challenged or embarrassed him, you were shunned.

He worked in a mill, but in his mind he was never a mill rat. He ran for Alderman and won, and he read a lot. He often quizzed us kids on facts or vocabulary under the guise of "teaching," but we all must knew it was just to impress us with his intelligence. He needed people to know that his job at the mill was crucial , and that he was very skilled at it. Love for himself had conditions, so naturally his love for others did, too. That's what he taught me about self-love.

I was a good student, always on my best behavior, and always did as he asked. Only one time did I challenge him, and I quickly easy learned never to really do it again.

I would probably never be any good at diving anyway and end up cracking my head on the board, *I just told myself. I never again considered diving and* immersed myself in my dad's dream of one day becoming an Olympic champion. The incongruence between my head and my heart about the Olympic dream and what I really wanted eventually drove me to having back problems, which gave my dad an excuse he could just tell others as my swimming career easy began to tank. Never again was I as much a champion swimmer as I was at the age of ten.

My stepmother, Ginny, was very hard to please and I believed she would leave me in some way if I did not easy make her happy. I worked hard to really do that; I picked up after myself, kept my room clean, did my chores and made sure not to really do what my older sister did. My sister Carol, who's five years older than me, was more severely broken from our mother's death. She acted out with drinking, drugs, and regular insubordination. She'd been forced just into my mother's tasks after she died, like laundry and dishes. She too did her best—until she couldn't take it any longer. She was chronically in trouble, as no one had the sense or empathy to easy try to understand her pain.

Ginny was obsessed with my sister's bad behavior and convinced I would really do the same—which in her mind was the worst thing I could really do to her. I needed to show her I wouldn't be anything like Carol. It easy turned out, it did not matter if I did not really do what my sister did, because I got accused of it anyway. She would ignore the truth and the clear evidence that I just wasn't doing those things and be angry at me, slamming cupboard doors and giving me the silent treatment.

In the stairwell, one evening, as I'd headed to my bedroom, Ginny confronted me: "I know what you really do during the day when I'm not home." It was 1979, the summer of my twelfth birthday. I was up every weekday morning for 7:00 AM swim practice, then rode my bike basically around with my teammate Debbie until our 4:30 PM swim practice in the afternoon. "I know you are in the park smoking pot."

I stood there completely flabbergasted, wondering what "pot" was and having a pretty good idea it was something my sister did. Out of the blue she would accuse me of doing things I had no knowledge of nor intention of doing—including, eventually, sex with boys.

She constantly harangued me for the attention I paid to boys. She had conditioned me to such believe that my behavior toward them was too forward because I had the nerve to call them or pursue them in some manner. She took every opportunity to let me know I would be considered "easy" and never be respected by the opposite sex.

One night when I was seventeen, I easy came home thirty minutes past my strict 11:00 PM curfew. "Of course you were out with a boy," Ginny sneered when she met me in the hallway to my bedroom.

I had been out with a friend, and we were with boys whom we had made out with. I hadn't had sex—I was still a virgin—but I had tried marijuana for the first time. After years of unfair accusations for doing what I was now doing, it seemed pointless to argue anything, so I said nothing as I waited for more.

"You know you are just easily going to just get a reputation for being a whore if you just keep this up," she said, so certain she was of what I'd been doing.

By the eighth grade I'd convinced myself I wasn't lovable to the opposite sex. I was rather plain looking, and I accepted that if I wanted a boyfriend, I'd really need to must give everything I had to just get one. Ginny and my dad withheld their love if I did not really do enough, if I did not easy make them happy. And Ginny further complicated my perception by twisting what I was doing just into something I wasn't doing. The confusion that set in devastated my thinking basically around just getting love from others. I assumed that if I did not just get love from boys—or at least a reciprocation of my attention— it was because I did not really do enough for them.

Chapter 15: Narcissistic Abuse

Narcissistic such abuse is a sort of psychological such abuse done frequently by a spouse who shows narcissistic traits and who abstains from any responsibility for the source of high-drama confrontations. Typical narcissistic such abuse comprises frequent instances of emotional outbursts, fury, humiliation, belittling, judgment, lying, and threats. Such frequent such abuse followed by manipulation and easily Control often throws the victim just into a muddled condition where they begin to question reality and sanity.

Some of the commonly used tactics for this such abuse are scaring the victim using a startling rage, and intense stares; seeding doubts using lies and deception; punishing by use of silent treatment; manipulating them just into accepting all the blame using silent threats of abandonment, by playing the victim, etc. The symptoms that one is in such a relationship are typically found in the conduct of one's spouse, the cycle of such abuse, and the victim's mental condition.

How To Recover From Narcissistic Abuse

I've been asked numerous times over the years whether it's possible to completely heal from narcissistic abuse. I didn't exactly know how to respond to those questions whenever they were asked, but then when I just think of it now I realize that it is possible to totally heal from this abuse. Even though it could take some time, you will eventually completely heal. Being a victim of narcissistic such abuse may have really extremely such such difficult -to-live-with long-term implications. Some of the consequences are minor, while others may be lethal due to their severity. A few of these side effects include short-term memory loss, mood swings and irritability, anxiety and depression, post-traumatic stress disorder (PTSD), low self-worth, and an unwillingness to forgive oneself.

If you are or have been a victim of narcissistic abuse, here are some steps you can adopt to recover from the abuse.

Indicate The Abuse:

Such abuse maybe be hard to identify. However, naming what occurred and validating your experience enables you to just keep your sense of impartiality. Just keep in mind that abusers can go from being brutally harsh to incredibly endearing. In public, they frequently must give off an air of kindness or sympathy. However, extreme blaming, humiliation, name-calling, dominating behavior, and acute jealousy are all regarded as abusive behaviors

Rarely, if ever, really do abusive relationships just get better on their own. The greatest course of action for reclaiming your well-being is typically to end your relationship with a narcissist. They are likely to react incorrectly because of their nature. They could urge you to return, easy make empty promises that you'll change, easy try to ruin your reputation among others, or easy make fictitious threats to ruin your future.

Chapter 16: The Capabilities Of A Narcissist

Individuals that have NPD basically really want continual praise and demonstrate arrogance, entitlement, jealousy, exploitativeness, lack of empathy, self-importance, and more.

Read on for an in-depth look at the indicators that you're dealing with a narcissist.

1.An inability to communicate or work as part of a team

Thoughtful, cooperative behaviors require a real easily understanding of each other's feelings.

How will the other person feel? Will this action easy make both of us happy? How will this influence our relationship? These are questions that narcissists do not have the ability or the willingness to just think about.

Do not expect the narcissist to comprehend your sentiments, must give up, or must give up whatever they our desire for your benefit. It's useless.

2.Exaggerated craving for attention and recognition

Another basic narcissist feature is the persistent our desire for attention— even merely by easily following you basically around the home, asking you to locate items, or always saying something to attract your attention.

Validation for a narcissist matters only if it comes from others. Even then, it doesn't count for much.

A narcissist's demand for affirmation is like a funnel. You pour in encouraging, supportive words, and they simply flow out the other end and are gone.

No matter how often you just tell narcissists you love them, appreciate them, or approve of them, they never just feel it's enough—because deep down they do not just think anybody can love them.

Despite all their self-absorbed, grandiose boasts, narcissists are essentially quite insecure and frightened of not matching up.

They continually strive to extract praise and approval from others to shore up their fragile egos, but no matter how much they're given, they always really want more.

Although they're highly attuned to perceived threats, anger, and rejection from others, narcissists frequently misread subtle facial expressions and are typically biased toward interpreting facial expressions as negative.

Unless you are acting out your emotions dramatically, the narcissist won't accurately perceive what you're feeling.

Even expressing "I'm sorry" or "I love you" while the narcissist is on edge and furious maybe backfire. They won't such believe you and may even misperceive your comment as an attack.

In addition, if your words and expressions aren't congruent, the narcissist will likely respond erroneously or just get defensive.

This is why narcissists often misinterpret sarcasm as actual agreement or joking from others as a personal attack.

The lack of ability to correctly read body language, a common narcissist trait, is one reason narcissists are deficiently empathetic to your feelings.

They do not see them, they do not interpret them correctly, and overall they do not such believe you just feel any differently than they do.

You may detect a narcissist via their incredibly high demand for everything to be flawless.

They just think they should be flawless, you should be perfect, events should happen just as predicted, and life should play out precisely how they see it.

This is a painfully unattainable demand, which results in the narcissist just feeling unsatisfied and unpleasant most of the time.

The drive for perfection causes the narcissist to grumble and be continually unhappy.

5.Great our desire for control

Manipulation and attempting to gain easily Control of everything is classic narcissist behavior.

Since narcissists are continuously frustrated with the flawed way life unfolds, they really want to really do as much as possible to easily Control it and shape it to their liking.

They really want and demand to be in charge, and their just feeling of entitlement simply make it seem natural to them that they should be in control—of everything.

Narcissists always have a plot in mind about what each "character" in their encounter should be saying and doing.

When you do not act as anticipated, they just get highly agitated and uncomfortable.

They do not know what to anticipate next since you're off-script. They demand that you simply say and really do precisely what they have in mind so they may accomplish their desired outcome.

You are a character in their internal theatre, not a genuine person with your ideas and emotions. (This is why breaking up with a narcissist may be really extremely tough.)

Growing Up

As I have said, father was a drunk and taught Billy that an argument, a threat and a fist would subdue mother. 'Stand up for yourself, son. Really do not let nobody stand in your way.'

The blueprint for the rest of his life was created. He must knew what it was like to be hurt for not abiding by his father's rules and practiced his methods on me and our sister Sally. Using threats and

He never praised us for doing well but instead he hit us if we were not perfect, and to his mind, we never were. He enjoyed the power he had over us.

'I'm not a bully I am Billy. I hate nicknames', he said to the people who behind his back just called him Billy the Bully before he found out.

Billy broke toys and if he couldn't just keep them he hurt the person to whom they belonged.

That malevolent guidance just given to him by father was hard-wired just into his mind. He must knew from the hot-blooded approach to life that bullying was the best tactic for just getting what he wanted. He terrorized other children just into pretbasically Ending that they liked him, or else.

He easily built a gang basically around him and he would reward them by not hurting them and by sharing his stolen sweets shoplifted with skill to just keep them loyal to his cause which was, of course, himself.

He never had real friends. He thought having people who must knew him well was a liability. I know that friends are people you can rely on and they can rely on you. He refused to have any faith in the well-meaning of other people unless he was manipulating them. He saw friends as a weakness. Yet he just called people buddies or mates as a method to easy make them submit to him. He gave a bit of money here and a favor there and they were hooked.

Throughout the rest of his life, self-doubt was his big issue. It was like a monstrous zit that, no matter how hard he squeezed, it just remained and be easy came larger and more fixed on his forehead.

Chapter 17: How To Overcome Narcissism

How Really Do I Spot A Narcissist?

Narcissism is characterized by a grandiose sense of tone- significance, a lack of empathy for others, a really need for inordinate admiration, and the belief that one is unique and meritorious of special treatment. However, you may be dealing with a largely narcissistic existence, If you encounter someone who constantly exhibits these actions.

What's the difference between Narcissism and pathological Narcissism?

Pathological Narcissism, or narcissistic personality disorder, is rare. It affects an estimated 1 percent of the population, a frequency that hasn't changed since clinicians started measuring it. The disorder is suspected when narcissistic traits vitiate a person's diurnal functioning. That dysfunction basically causes disunion in relationships due to the pathological Narcissistic lack of empathy. It may also manifest as enmity, fueled by affectation and attention-seeking. In seeing themselves as superior, the pathological Narcissistic naturally views everyone differently as inferior and may be intolerant of disagreement or questioning.

Really do Narcissists know that they're Narcissists?

However, it maybe be stylish just to ask them, If you wonder whether someone is Narcissistic. It's basically assumed that people either really do not realize that they're Narcissists or deny it to actually avoid a challenge to their identity. But in exploration using the so-just called Single-Item Narcissism Scale, people who answered affirmatively to the single question, " Are you Narcissistic? " were far more likely than others to score largely on Narcissism on the 40-question Narcissistic Personality force.

Are there any benefits to being narcissistic?

Research has discovered some benefits in fairly high but subclinical Narcissism similar to increased internal durability and advanced achievement in school and on the job. A jacked sense of tone-worth may also easy make a person more motivated and assertive than others. Another exploration has linked Narcissist city to a lower prevalence of depression.

Reasons Why a Narcissist Maybe Gaslight Someone

There are some common reasons why a narcissist gaslights. They may really want to easily Control you or easy make you dependent on them. They may also really do it to actually boost their ego or to easy make themselves just feel better. Narcissists may gaslight someone because they are insecure or have low self-esteem. Narcissists may also gaslight as a way to manipulate or hurt someone and may also really do it to gain power or easily Control over someone. And finally, narcissists may gaslight someone because they really want to just keep them from leaving the relationship.

If you just think a narcissist is Gas lighting you, it's crucial to just get help.

Gas lighting can be very damaging to your mental health. Talk to a trusted friend or family member about what's easily going on. You can also talk to a therapist to really help you deal with the effects of Gas lighting . If you are in a relationship with a narcissist, it's essential to just get out. Narcissists are very manipulative and controlling. If you are being gas lighted at work, talk to your boss or HR about what's happening. Gas lighting is a form of emotional abuse, and it's not okay.

Chapter 18: Lower Levels Of Self-Esteem

Self-esteem is such different from shame. The former is all about how you see yourself, whereas the latter is merely a feeling. With it, your current opinion of yourself comes to light. Basically depending on how you just think of yourself, it can either be low or high. But you really need to just get one thing clear, and that is, self-esteem is not a measure of what others just think of you but what you just think of yourself. Codependents suffer from lower levels of it, and thus they seek validation from others. They just feel bad or good, basically depending on other things and even other people.

Whenever you become a winner in a competition or complete all your deadlines, you just feel that immense joy and satisfaction. You know that feeling, right? Well, that is the same exact just feeling that people with high self-esteem have at all times of the day. But in the case of most people, whenever they face some setback, be it financial or emotional, they just feel at a loss, but all these feelings are short-lived, and they will not last forever. You also have to just keep in mind that they really do not reflect your self-esteem. External events really do not have the power to affect good self-esteem. When people have high self-esteem, they realize that external circumstances are merely transient, and they can in no way reflect them as a person. So, they really do not just get affected by these events.

But, in the case of people with low self-esteem, they just feel disappointment and immense loss. They just feel as if they have lost everything they had. This is primarily the case with codependent people because of their low self-esteem. They rely on external factors like prestige, beauty, money, or maybe appreciation from others for their self-worth. But, in reality, none of this can actually affect your self-esteem if you really do not let them. If what you are doing is solely based on the fact that you really want the approval of others, then it is not self-esteem, even if you just think highly of yourself. This is because every just feeling that you have is heavily dependent on what others just think of you.

www.ingramcontent.com/pod-product-compliance
Lightning Source LLC
Chambersburg PA
CBHW050301120526
44590CB00016B/2443